D1709083

FIRST BIOGRAPHIES

Sandra Day O'Connor

Published by Raintree Steck-Vaughn Publishers, an imprint of Steck-Vaughn Company

Planned and produced by The Creative Publishing Company
Editors: Christine Lawrie and Pam Wells

Library of Congress Cataloging-in-Publication Data

Holland, Gini.
Sandra Day O'Connor / Gini Holland; illustrated by Gary Rees.
p. cm. — (First biographies)
Summary: Introduces the life and accomplishments of the first woman to be named to the Supreme Court.
ISBN 0-8172-4455-7
1. O'Connor, Sandra Day, 1930- — Juvenile literature. 2. United States. Supreme Court — Biography — Juvenile literature. 3. Women judges — United States — Biography — Juvenile literature.
4. O'Connor, Sandra Day, 1930- . [1. United States. Supreme Court — Biography. 2. Judges. 3. Women — Biography.] I. Rees, Gary, ill.
II. Title. III. Series.
KF8745.O25H65 1997
347.73'2634 — dc20
[B]
[347.3073534] 96-19996
[B] CIP
AC

Printed and bound in the United States
1 2 3 4 5 6 7 8 9 0 W 01 00 99 98 97

FIRST BIOGRAPHIES

Sandra Day O'Connor

Gini Holland
Illustrated by Gary Rees

RAINTREE STECK-VAUGHN PUBLISHERS
The Steck-Vaughn Company
Austin, Texas

Sandra Day O'Connor was the first woman justice on the Supreme Court of the United States. The Supreme Court is where arguments about what the laws of the country mean are settled by nine judges, or justices. The Presidents of the United States choose these judges. Until President Reagan chose Sandra Day O'Connor in 1981, no President, in over two hundred years, had ever chosen a woman.

Sandra Day was born on March 26, 1930. When she was growing up, Sandra's family lived on their ranch in Arizona, near the border of New Mexico. Her grandfather started the ranch in the 1870s. He dug wells, set up windmills, and then bought cattle from Mexico. These cattle were branded with a letter "B" lying on its side, so he named his ranch the "Lazy B."

As a very young child, Sandra had no playmates except farm animals, cats, and cowboys. But she learned how to amuse herself. One way was to collect all the kittens and cats that lived in the barns. She became very angry with her father one time. She found out he had taken some of them to a distant pasture to fend for themselves.

Sandra's parents were well-educated. Her mother taught Sandra to read by the time she was four years old. Reading became her favorite hobby. When she was five, her parents sent her to live with her Grandmother and Grandfather Wilkey in El Paso, Texas. This way, Sandra could get a good education. She came home to the ranch for vacations.

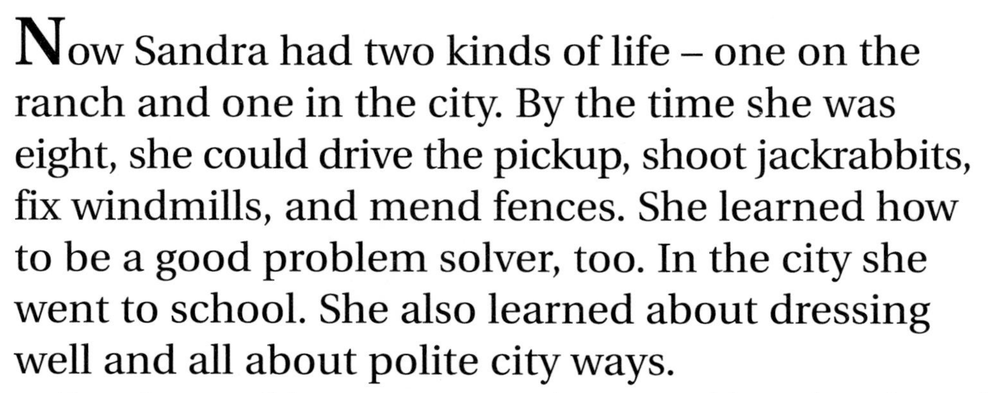

Now Sandra had two kinds of life – one on the ranch and one in the city. By the time she was eight, she could drive the pickup, shoot jackrabbits, fix windmills, and mend fences. She learned how to be a good problem solver, too. In the city she went to school. She also learned about dressing well and all about polite city ways.

Sandra and her younger sister and brother loved their summers on the ranch. They rode their horses every day and swam in the water tank to cool off. They hated to leave at the end of the vacations.

Once, at the end of summer, Sandra and her cousin Flournoy refused to come out of the water tank. They did not want to go back to school. Sandra's father got a lariat, the kind of rope he used to catch stray cows. Laughing, he roped them out of the water.

Sandra was so good in school that she skipped two grades. She graduated from high school when she was only sixteen. Her father had not been able to go to Stanford University, in California, as he had wanted to years before. Sadly, his father had died, and he had to take over the ranch. But now, in 1946, Sandra could go. She studied hard and got good grades, as usual.

Still she had time for her friends, too. Her father remembers, "She used to bring a bunch of girls from Stanford for the spring roundup, and I'd tell her, 'Sandra, I don't have time to be saddling horses for a bunch of sissies,' but you know, those kids just took care of themselves pretty well."

Sandra met her future husband, John Jay O'Connor III, while working on the *Stanford Law Review* together. He was another law student. They liked each other right away and had dinner together the day they met.

Sandra graduated with the third highest grades in her class of 102 graduates. John still had one year to go, but they decided to get married. They were both twenty-two years old.

Sandra and John were married on December 20, 1952, in a brand new barn at the Lazy B ranch. John was the son of a San Francisco doctor. He did not know much about ranch life. "I've seen better cowboys," Sandra's father teased him. But Sandra's mother said that if Sandra had been looking for a cowboy, she would not have gone looking at Stanford University.

Sandra was ready to start work as a lawyer, while John finished law school. But no California law firm would hire her because she was a woman. It was not that the men in law firms in those days hated women. Most of them just never thought about a woman working as a real lawyer. It did not fit their ideas of how the world was supposed to be. Finally, she landed a job as a deputy county attorney.

CALIFORNIA REPUBLIC

In 1957, John was hired by a law firm in Phoenix, Arizona. Sandra would have a chance to move back to her home state. It was a busy time. On October 5, both Sandra and her husband were sworn in as lawyers in the state of Arizona. On October 8, she gave birth to their first son, Scott. The following year, she and another lawyer started their own law firm.

Sandra and John bought some land outside Phoenix. Here, they built their home themselves. They even soaked each adobe brick in skim milk to give it a special shine.

Sandra Day O'Connor was not just a working woman. Her second son, Brian, was born in 1960. She took time off from work for five years to take care of the children while they were little. During this time, in 1962, her third son, Jay, was born. But she still managed to find time to do volunteer work.

In 1969, Sandra became a state senator. She made speeches, and people liked what she said. In 1973, as a Republican, she became leader of the majority party in the state senate. She was the first woman to lead her political party in a state senate.

She was very careful with public money. She was good at listening to people's ideas, even when they were different from her own. This is called being "open-minded." She was also very fair.

In 1974, Sandra ran for Arizona Superior Court Judge for Maricopa County. She promised to be firm with lawbreakers and won the election, taking office in 1975. She quickly became known as a “no-nonsense” person who handed out strict punishment to criminals. People liked her strength and fairness.

In the mid-1970s, Arizona Republican leaders asked her to think about running for governor. She would be running against the Democrat, Bruce Babbitt, who was then governor of Arizona. She decided not to run. In 1979, Governor Babbitt appointed her to the Arizona Court of Appeals. Each time she was serving on a higher court.

Many voters were starting to ask for more women in government. When Ronald Reagan ran for President, he promised that he would choose a woman to fill "one of the first vacancies on the Supreme Court in my administration."

In 1981, he got his chance. Justice Potter Stewart gave up his job that summer. President Reagan nominated Sandra Day O'Connor for the United States Supreme Court.

The President can nominate, or name, his choice, but the U.S. Senate has to approve it. The eighteen U.S. senators on the Senate Judiciary Committee asked Sandra tough questions for hours and hours. In the end, they liked what she had to say. All but one voted for her appointment to the Supreme Court.

Justice O'Connor and her family now live in Washington, D.C., full-time. Justice O'Connor is a hard worker. She often works twelve-hour days. Thousands of cases reach the Supreme Court every year. This is more than the nine justices have time to listen to. So they have to meet together and choose the most important ones.

Many people expected Justice O'Connor to be a very strict judge. But some of the decisions she has made have surprised them.

Justice O'Connor hopes most people never have to go to court. She tells us to, "...remember the golden rule: do unto others what you would have them do unto you. That might make you a little more generous, save you a lot of time and money, and make my job a lot easier."

Key Dates

1930 Born in El Paso, Texas, on March 26.

1950 Graduates from Stanford University.

1952 Was the third-best student out of 102 at Stanford Law School. Marries John Jay O'Connor III on December 20.

1957 Settles in Phoenix, Arizona, with her husband. Sandra and husband are both sworn in as lawyers in the state of Arizona on October 5. Gives birth to first of her three sons.

1958 Sets up private law practice with family friend Tom Tobin.

1960 Gives birth to her second son. Takes a leave from the law practice to raise her sons.

1962 Gives birth to her third son.

1969 Appointed by Maricopa County Board of Supervisors to fill vacancy as a state senator.

1973 Becomes the first woman to lead her political party in a state senate.

1975 Takes oath of office as Maricopa County Superior Court Judge.

1979 Appointed to the Arizona Court of Appeals.

1981 Sworn in as Justice of the United States Supreme Court on September 25. She was the first woman ever appointed to the Supreme Court.